John

Freeman

D1291960

Your Family Worship Guidebook

Your Family Worship Guidebook

Reuben Herring

BROADMAN PRESS
Nashville, Tennessee

To my parents
John Greene Herring
and
Ruby Hewitt Herring
who taught me to worship

Scripture quotations marked (NASB) are from the *New American Standard* Bible. Copyright © The Lockman Foundation, 1960, 1962, 1963, 1971, 1972, 1973, 1975. Used by permission.

© Copyright 1978 · Broadman Press
All rights reserved.
4256–27
ISBN: 0–8054–5627–9
Dewey Decimal Classification: 249
Subject heading: FAMILY—RELIGIOUS LIFE//WORSHIP
Library of Congress Catalog Card Number: 78–19976
Printed in the United States of America.

Contents

1
The Why
of Family Worship

1
The Why
of Family Worship

We were trying to make the Bible "come alive" for our small children by dramatizing some of the exciting stories of the Old Testament. This time the story was of David and Goliath.

Drawing on all my limited dramatic resources, I stood in the middle of the den floor and silently pantomimed the actions of little David as he took a smooth stone from his pouch, placed it in his sling, and then rushed forward and hurled the stone with deadly accuracy at the head of the giant Goliath.

Then dramatically reversing my position on the den floor, I became Goliath. I clasped a hand to my forehead, sagged on wobbly knees, and fell to the floor.

Proud of my performance and confident that no one who had ever heard the story before could fail to interpret my actions, I raised up from the floor and asked my wide-eyed audience, "All right, who was that?"

Quick as a flash, our eight-year-old replied, "Matt Dillon, United States Marshal!"

While I am convinced of the effectiveness of active participation in family worship, I must admit that it does not always achieve the desired results. But I find some comfort in the knowledge that this kind of involvement in family worship has had a longer "run" at our house than the famous marshal of television.

A Definition

To worship is to recognize the supreme worth of God and to rejoice in his greatness. To worship is to do over and over again what we first did when we yielded our lives to God through Jesus Christ.

Family worship in the home is a natural outgrowth of man's need to worship, for the home is an even older religious institution than the church. The Jewish home has been deeply religious for centuries, and the spiritual unity of the family has been a strength of the Jewish people. The ancient Shema instructed Hebrew parents: "These words, which I command thee this day, shall be in thine heart: and thou shalt teach them diligently unto thy children, and shalt talk of them when thou sittest in thine house, and when thou walkest by the way, and when thou liest down, and when thou risest up" (Deut. 6:6–7).

Just as learning is most effective when the lesson the child is taught at school is reinforced at home, so the religious instruction of the church must be supported by the home.

When a child grows up in a home where there is little or no worship he is almost certain to conclude that worship is only for certain places and certain occasions. He may decide that religion is only for a particular part of life, to be put on and taken off like Sunday clothes. He may infer that religion and worship are only for the professional clergy, the priests and preachers, and not a part of everyday life of the average person.

Is a child capable of joining the family in worship? Certainly there is much about the experience of worship that is beyond the comprehension of a child, but no normal parent would tell his child not to go near the water until he learns to swim. Neither do we wait until the child can count calories before we give him a balanced diet. It is better for a child to have an unbalanced diet than for him to starve, and it is better for a child to be exposed to worship before he is ready to absorb all of it than to get nothing at all. Thomas Carlyle said, "When one begins to worship, he begins to grow." The child's need to worship is as great as his need to grow.

For the wisest counsel regarding children and worship, we must go to the ultimate authority, Jesus: "Permit the children to come to Me; do not hinder them; for the kingdom of God belongs to such as these. Truly I say to you, whoever does not receive the kingdom of God like a child shall not enter it *at all*" (Mark 10:14–15, NASB).

An Attitude

In family worship, as in other forms of worship, there is danger that the experience may become nothing more than an empty ritual. Too often a Sunday morning worship service is no more than this. It is the responsibility of parents to make worship in the home meaningful. Family worship should provide the opportunity for commitment of life to God.

Worship in the home is more meaningful when it is related naturally to daily living. This is true of all worship experiences. One of the strengths of worship in the home is that it can be related naturally and easily to the daily life of the family.

The attitude of family worship is the attitude of Joshua, that bold warrior of Israel: "As for me and my house, we will serve the Lord" (Josh. 24:15). Faithful, reverent worship in the home is one way a family can declare its allegiance to God.

A Resolve

As our family discovered in my attempt to panto-mime David slaying Goliath, not every attempt at worship in the home will be successful. Neither does a worship experience follow every time that a congregation assembles at eleven o'clock on Sunday morning. But if attempts to commune with God through worship are scheduled regularly, either at home or at church, results will follow.

There must be a firm resolve on the part of the family to seek faithfully to worship God and to leave the results in his hands. If a family resolves that "our house shall be a house of prayer," much of the battle is won. This commitment to be faithful in worship gives the undertaking a momentum that will carry the family along from day to day.

A major reason for the sporadic church attendance of millions is that many families have never made a commitment to be faithful in keeping the Lord's Day holy. If a family must decide each Sunday morning whether they will attend worship services, most of the time they will decide not to make the effort. Excuses come too readily: they overslept, they have nothing to wear, someone has a cold or a headache, weather conditions seem unfavorable. On the other hand, the family that has made a commitment to be faithful in church attendance never has to make any of these decisions. They know a full week in advance that, unless providentially hindered, they will be in church the following Sunday.

The same principle applies to family worship in the

home. Obstacles to worship in the home are countless: television, telephone, homework, housework, visitors, appointments, sickness, delays, interruptions, daily pressures. But the family that has made a firm resolve to be faithful in worship despite the obstacles will win the struggle. The family that must decide each day, "Shall we try to have family worship today or not?" is defeated before it starts.

A Time

It is no accident that the overwhelming majority of all churches of all denominations throughout the country observe the same worship hour: eleven o'clock on Sunday morning. No matter what part of the country a traveler is in, he can be reasonably certain that at eleven o'clock on Sunday morning he can enter a church and find a worship service about to begin.

The conditioning effect of a fixed time of worship, whether at church or at home, is powerful. The family that never begins a meal without first offering a prayer of thanks for the food establishes an attitude and a behavior pattern which children of that family will never quite outgrow. The family that fixes a time for worship also reaps dividends.

Most persons prefer to begin the day with worship. This is the ideal time for many. To "meet the Lord in the morning" helps to give direction and purpose to the entire day and to bless it with God's presence.

For many families, though, worship in the morning is out of the question. Father may be up and gone to work before the children are awake. Mother may be on yet another schedule. Older children may be on still another morning schedule and younger children on a fourth timetable. For such a family, early morning may be the most chaotic time of day.

Each family must find the time for worship that best fits its own needs. This time may be the first thing in the morning, the last thing at night, or somewhere in between. Probably this time cannot be determined without some experimentation. But when the most convenient hour is found (the time which is most conducive to worship for all the family), it should be established in the family routine and respected by all members.

A Place

Many religious families have a shrine or altar in the home which is the designated place of worship. Here religious symbols and other aids for worship are placed and used in worship.

Evangelicals generally regard altars and religious symbols as artificial or as identified with pagan worship, and shun their use. Yet even evangelical groups recognize the value of a fixed place of worship—that is why they build churches!

There is also value in a place of worship in the home. Here the Bible and other worship aids may be placed for ready use. This eliminates the need for searching the house for worship resources when the family is assembled. This place should be selected carefully in an area of the home as far removed as possible from the television, telephone, and other distractions.

An Occasion

The emphasis on the value of a fixed time and place for worship in the home does not rule out the need for moments of spontaneous worship by the family. Scarcely a week passes without some significant family experience that can be transformed into a moment of worship. A birthday, a holiday, a vacation, a long journey, homecoming, graduation, first day in school, a new job, a promotion, a raise in pay, the completion of a new house, a wedding, a conversion, a baptism, a sunrise, a flower, a bird's song, illness, death—all these events may become the center of family worship. Any one of these events or experiences can command the attention of the entire family. This attention can be directed to God as he is invited to share with the family in the moment of worship.

Years ago our family attended the football games of one of the local high schools because our oldest son was on the squad. As the parents and the two younger brothers of the football hero waited for the first game to begin, all of us were tense with excitement. Just before the opening kickoff, the youngest boy leaned over to his mother and said, "Don't you think we should have a prayer that no one gets hurt?"

We felt a strong sense of family togetherness and worship as we bowed quietly in that yelling crowd and prayed for the players. It became a family tradition with us. There are countless moments such as this when the family that is sensitive to these opportunities can worship naturally and spontaneously. God seems very near in those moments.

A Leader

Family worship requires a leader, but this does not mean that the same person should lead every worship experience. Better results are obtained if leadership responsibility is shared by every member of the family. Every parent who has ever taught a Sunday School class knows that the teacher learns the most as the class studies the Bible. The teacher makes the most careful preparation and is most intent on achieving the learning outcome. This principle also applies to the one who leads family worship. Usually the worship leader benefits most from the worship experience.

Even young children can share the responsibility for leading worship in the home. The child may be too young to read, but he can teach the family a song or Bible verse he knows, and he can lead in prayer and other worship activities.

Older children and youth make excellent leaders of family worship. With encouragement from parents, they can become highly creative and innovative in leading worship. These extraordinary worship experiences may be the most meaningful the family has. The responsibility of leading the family in worship helps children and youth toward spiritual maturity.

A Sponsor

While leadership responsibility in worship is best shared, one person must assume the role of sponsor. This person leads the family to begin family worship and then sees to it that the practice is faithfully maintained. He is an initiator, an encourager, and one who prods and reminds.

Make no mistake about it, there will be obstacles to overcome and discouragements to rise above if family worship is to continue. The sponsor will lead the family to be faithful to its commitment. He will be firm when the family falters in its resolve.

Leadership in family worship should be shared, but everyone's job is no one's job. The sponsor will help to protect the time and place of family worship, remind worship leaders of their duties, and see that schedules are maintained.

Ideally, this sponsor should be a parent or some other adult. However, a youth or older child can assume this role if adults in the family are lukewarm in their commitment to family worship. Best results usually are obtained when the husband and father accepts the role of sponsor. When the man of the house is also a priest before God to all his family, blessings flow to every member, particularly to the man.

A Lesson

Some students of worship and religious education maintain that worship is only a time to praise and glorify God and not a teaching-learning experience. The primary objective of worship is to glorify God, but religious education is a treasure gained as a by-product of the experience. In fact, it is difficult to separate worship from religious education. It is almost impossible to have one without the other.

As family members worship together in the home, they learn to understand and appreciate the Bible as the Word of God and to interpret and apply its truths to their lives. They learn the language of prayer and how to communicate with God. They are drawn closer together and closer to God in the worship experience and develop the graces of love, understanding, patience, forgiveness, repentance, humility, kindness, unselfishness, and other qualities that enrich and ennoble family life.

What parents must guard against is the temptation to use family worship to manipulate or coerce. Family worship is not the time when parents review all the

child's transgressions, past and present, and instruct
him to pray that God will help to make him a better
child. Rather, it is a time when parents and child alike
humble themselves before God, confess their faults to
one another, and pray for one another.

In family worship, a parent may confess to his child
that he has sinned against the child, seek the child's
forgiveness, and then pray for God's forgiveness and
restoration. From experiences such as this, revival can
come to family life.

A Spirit

Jesus said, "Where two or three are gathered together in my name, there am I in the midst of them"
(Matt. 18:20). This is the spirit of family worship. It is
the family acknowledging the presence of the Lord
in their midst and seeking his guidance as they honor
him in the home.

The family that worships recognizes that "except the
Lord build the house, they labour in vain that build
it" (Ps. 127:1). Without the presence and power of the
Holy Spirit, all attempts at worship in the home will
be futile. The family must plan and work and evaluate
their worship experiences and then start the process
all over again. But all this is done with a conscious
dependence upon the Holy Spirit to direct.

"Not by might, nor by power, but by my spirit, saith
the Lord" (Zech. 4:6). Family worship in the home
can be a dramatic testing ground for the truth of these
words. No one else on earth besides the members of
the family may know that the family gathers faithfully
for worship in the home. Those few minutes given regularly to worship may seem insignificant. But the unseen Presence who has promised to be in the midst

of that tiny circle can take those feeble, stumbling efforts at worship and produce results that will stand throughout eternity.

A Method

Praise and adoration of God; the reading, interpretation, and application of the Scriptures; meditation, reflection, self-examination, commitment, prayer—these are some of the major elements of family worship. Each member of the family, according to his age, ability, and experience, should demonstrate skills in these elements of worship.

Activity–centered worship is the method recommended here to help family members develop their worship skills. Educators have conducted experiments which indicate the following results:

The learner retains 10 percent of what he reads.
He retains 20 percent of what he hears.
He retains 30 percent of what he sees.
He retains 50 percent of what he sees and hears.
He retains 70 percent of what he speaks in conversation.
The learner retains 90 percent of what he speaks in conversation during a learning activity.

The power of the learning activity is that it requires a response from the learner. If his senses of hearing, sight, feeling, smell, and taste can be involved in the activity, his response is even stronger. A learner remembers painful experiences—the hot stove, the paddle. He also remembers pleasant experiences when his senses and emotions are rewarded.

The methodology of this approach to family worship is to involve all members of the family in a worship

experience. Their senses and emotions will be stirred.
They will be led to act and to respond. The total effect
will be a pleasant, memorable experience. Family worship will be associated with the closeness and harmony
of family fun—for that is what it is. But this fun will
have the added dimension of worship.

No one can read the Psalms without sensing the
psalmist's feelings of joy, exhilaration, even hilarity.
It is the same sense of joy in worship that this approach
to family worship seeks to recapture.

A Goal

Each experience in family worship should have a
desired outcome or goal. Without this sense of direction
and purpose, worship may become aimless and wan-
dering. In addition to this goal for each worship experience, there should be an overarching goal for family
worship. This long-range goal may be as modest or
ambitious as the family chooses to make it.

For the family just beginning family worship, their
long-range goal may be something like "our house shall
be a house of prayer." This is simply a goal to establish
family worship as a regular practice in the home.

A more ambitious goal for the family with more experience in worship might be that each member of the
family will demonstrate improved skills in worship.
Then the family will determine how to measure these
improved skills. These skills might include knowledge
of the Bible, Bible reading, interpretation and application of the Bible, growth in prayer and meditation,
greater self-understanding, mature worship insights,
and the like.

Progress toward these long-range goals should be
evaluated periodically. As this evaluation of family wor-

ship is made annually or more often, these and other questions might be answered:

Are we faithful in worship?

Is a time and place for worship established?

Are all members of the family involved in the worship experiences?

Is leadership responsibility shared by family members?

Are praise and adoration, Bible interpretation and application, prayer and meditation, reflection and self-examination, commitment, and other basic elements of worship included?

Are family members demonstrating greater skills in worship?

A Prayer

Is this emphasis upon involvement of all the family in worship activities too mechanical? Will something be lost if the family experiments with a new approach to worship in the home?

Perhaps these questions can be answered best with other questions. Has something been lost from worship since our forefathers worshiped on the American frontier a century or two ago? Was worship more effective when families gathered in a clearing or under a brush arbor rather than in a church? Was preaching more effective when it was done once a month or less often rather than every week? Were worship services better held only in daylight and when work and weather did not hinder rather than day and night, regardless of the weather or other hindrances? Was church leadership more capable when it was done by untrained frontiersmen rather than by seminary-trained pastors? Was the church program more productive when it centered around irregular preaching only rather than a multifaceted program that challenges the interests and enlists the talents of many people?

The answer to these questions is that our forefathers probably did the best they could with what they had and longed for a better day. It is to their credit that when advanced methods of reaching people with the gospel were introduced, most of them adopted these innovations over the protests of the minority. We should not forget that a few generations ago a highly vocal minority in the churches vigorously opposed such standard practices of today as Sunday Schools, seminaries, musical instruments, publishing boards, and even foreign mission programs.

As we try a new tack in family worship, our prayer might be that we will have the courage and foresight of those who have gone before us. They were not afraid to try new methods and strategies, even when some warned of dire consequences. They put new approaches to the test. If the new measured up to the test, they adopted it. If it failed, they discarded it in favor of the old until something better could be found.

The God who is the same yesterday and today and forever has said, "Behold, I make all things new" (Rev. 21:5). With him we can seek new horizons in family worship. May he richly bless you in your undertaking.

2
The How
of Family Worship

2
The How
of Family Worship

Memories of my early childhood include experiences in family worship, or "family altar" as we called it. Significantly, I was grown before I understood the term.

Our large family of nine usually gathered around the supper table for worship. Father or Mother would read a passage from the Bible, usually without comment, and then one or the other of them would pray. Sometimes each of us in turn prayed around the family circle, but we smaller children were asleep long before our turn came to pray. An older brother or sister would nudge the sleeping child, he would lift his head from the table groggily, mutter a few words, and then drop back to sleep on the table. Even when only Father or Mother prayed, we were usually sound asleep long before the "amen."

At other times, perhaps in a desperate attempt to keep the smaller children awake, we would memorize Bible verses. We committed to memory such pearls of wisdom as, "Why beholdest thou the mote that is in thy brother's eye, but considerest not the beam that is in thine own eye?" (Matt. 7:3); "Blessed are the poor in spirit: for theirs is the kingdom of heaven" (Matt. 5:3); "Blessed are they which do hunger and thirst after righteousness: for they shall be filled" (Matt. 5:6); "Give not that which is holy unto the dogs, neither cast ye your pearls before swine" (Matt. 7:6); "But when thou doest alms, let not thy left hand know what thy right hand doeth" (Matt. 6:3).

We memorized faithfully, and I can still quote some of the verses I learned almost a half century ago. But it was almost a quarter of a century after I learned the verses before I had even the vaguest notion of what the words meant.

Was this childhood experience completely devoid of meaning? Were the tireless efforts of my parents wasted? Not at all. The words that were "hidden in my heart" many years ago are still there. The experience has some value for me because I wanted to continue the practice of family worship with my own children. But how much more valuable the experience would have been if it had been communicated to me on my own level of interest and understanding!

The prophet Amos asked, "Can two walk together, except they be agreed?" (3:3). If parent and child are to walk together, the parent must slow his pace to match the pace of the child. The child can run to keep up for awhile—as children often do when they chase after their parents on a busy sidewalk. But soon the child tires and falls far behind.

If families are to worship together, the parent must match his pace to that of the child. Even the older child must slow his pace to that of the younger child. The younger child must match the pace of the toddler.

This does not mean that family worship must always move at a snail's pace. Each can respond and worship on his own level of understanding. But the older worshiper must always keep in mind the needs and interests of the younger and make provision for him.

Talking It Over

People who study the family have found one event in the everyday life of the family that seems to have more influence on children than any other single experience. That event is mealtime.

When the family is relaxed around the dining table, words, attitudes, and behavior are expressed that have profound effect on children. Many a parent has preoccupied himself with putting food on the table, unaware that what went on around the table was fully as important as what was put on the table.

Our Lord, no doubt, was aware of the unifying effect of "breaking bread together" as he instituted the Lord's Supper. As he did so, he built upon the powerful efficacy already present in the observance of the Passover meal.

Because of the influence of mealtime on family members, the decline of this daily ritual is cause for alarm. Rare is the family that gathers for three meals a day, and many families do not sit down together for even one meal a day. The demands of a fast-paced, mobile society make it increasingly difficult for the family to gather for meals. Mothers who work outside the home have less time to prepare meals for the family. The rapidly growing number of quick food outlets, now almost as numerous as service stations, further attest to the decline of family mealtimes.

Family mealtime gives the family opportunity to sit down together and quietly discuss the events of the day and other matters of interest and concern to family members. Of course families do not always sit quietly and calmly discuss events. Mealtime often is a confusion of interruptions, arguments, reprimands, and heated debates. Ideally, however, the family at least has opportunity for fruitful discussion.

Family worship also provides opportunity for discussion. The family not only will read a Bible passage but also they will talk about what it means and how its truths may be applied to daily living. As the family engages in activities related to worship, they will share feelings and attitudes about these matters.

Few parents need to be reminded of how quickly children grow up. It seems that as soon as they learn to tie their shoes, they are gone, and there is so much left undone and unsaid. One day the nest is empty, and the parents who are left behind suddenly realize that they never had a conversation with their children in which they discussed anything more profound than fashions or football. There always seemed to be plenty of time for those "serious talks" that every parent intends to have with his child before the child is on his own.

Family worship provides a structure for these conversations. Even for those families fortunate enough to have mealtimes together regularly, usually the table conversation seldom gets beyond the trivia of daily living—weather, politics, health, family budget, school, work, neighbors, friends. Family worship, however, provides a natural setting for talk about eternal verities—life, death, heaven, hell, faith, love, truth, freedom, God, man, sin, and salvation.

Family Dynamics

There is a dynamic in family life, particularly when the family is at worship, to be found nowhere else. Family relationships are unique. We borrow the terms for family relationships and apply them elsewhere—

"like a father to me," "sisters under the skin," "soul brother," "she mothered him"—but these ties are not the same. Blood ties are deep, and when these ties are further strengthened by family worship experiences in the home, the strength of the Christian family becomes apparent.

A mathematical equation may be used to express the relationships possible in a family. The equation is expressed: $n(n-1) = x$. When the family is composed of only husband and wife, only two relationships are possible: $2(2-1) = 2$. But when a child is born, there are not three possible relationships but six! This is expressed: $3(3-1) = 6$. Thus, in my own family of seven (five children and two parents) there are forty-two different relationships constantly at work. And in my father's family of nine there are seventy-two relationships! These relationships may be seen graphically by drawing a circle of nine dots (representing nine family members), linking each dot with all the other dots, and then counting the number of lines linking the dots.

This multiplicity of family relationships and possible interactions helps explain the complexity of family life. The arrival of the first child does not add another relationship but triples the number of relationships possible when the husband and wife were childless. A second child increases the number of interactions by six times!

These interactions are also a strength of family life. When family interaction is positive and affirming rather than negative and destructive, family members grow into healthy, mature persons. Bring these same dynamic family interactions to family worship, and the results are even more rewarding.

Following the Discussion

The basic methodology of this approach to family worship is simple: Scripture reading, discussion, and response. Each event builds upon the other to strengthen and reinforce learning.

There is value in the family's gathering to read from the Bible. This was the simple approach used by my parents. A child learns from this experience. He senses that this Book and this moment are important because of the value accorded the Bible and family worship by his parents.

Bible reading may be reinforced by a discussion of the meaning of the passage. Parents and children may ask questions and together seek answers. When the family cannot agree on the meaning of a passage, Bible study aids may be used to reach agreement. An important part of this discussion is in deciding how family members will apply the biblical truths and insights in daily life.

In response, family members act upon what they have read and talked about, further reinforcing the worship experience. This action response is particularly helpful for children. They may not understand the reading, and much of the discussion may be over their heads. But when they respond on their own level of comprehension, positive learning results.

Suppose the Scripture passage is Luke 10:25-37, the story of the good Samaritan. After the passage is read, the family discusses its meaning and application. This learning is reinforced as family members stage an impromptu skit, acting out the parts of the persons in the story.

Learning may be further enriched if the family applies the truth of the passage by showing kindness and compassion to someone in need. If this follow-up experience is linked with the Bible story of the Samaritan, even preschoolers can grasp the truth of the passage.

Response and application are steps frequently missing from religious education. A preacher's sermon may be carefully prepared and forcefully delivered, but few in the congregation can recall much, if any, of the sermon the following Sunday. The mind wanders too easily if the hearer does not actively respond.

In family worship, parents follow up reading of the Bible with discussion. But this discussion may fail to reach the child's level, or parents may do all the talking. In response and application, though, the child becomes involved as he acts upon what he has heard.

Following are some of the learning activities families may use to enrich family worship.

Games

This is a favorite activity of children and one of the most effective teaching methods with preschoolers. Some added benefits of games in family worship are that they help to make the experience more enjoyable for the child and draw parent and child closer together. Fortunate is the child whose parents take time to play with him!

Pantomime or charades—The method I used with such laughable results to depict the story of David and Goliath. Exaggerated movements and facial expressions are used to tell a story without words.

Skit—A simple dramatization performed with or without rehersal, costumes, and props.

Puzzle—Players search for missing words, names, or other clues.

Guessing game—Certain clues are provided and participants try to guess the partially identified Bible character, place, or thing.

Listening game—Participants listen for certain words, meanings, or other clues to answer questions already asked about the story.

Jigsaw—Participants fit together jumbled parts of a picture or other puzzle.

Communication game—This game tests powers of concentration and observation. In one version, a whispered message is passed around the family circle to see if the last member receives the original message.

Hide and seek—Every child loves this game. Some clue related to the worship experience is hidden and family members look for it.

Pretend—Another game in which children excel. Family members may pretend they are Bible characters or are participating in a Bible event.

Group Activities

Case study—Participants analyze a hypothetical case related to the worship experience.

Question and answer—To vary this activity, let the children ask the questions and the parents provide answers.

Circular response—Each member in turn responds to a question or statement.

Reaction slips—This is similar to the circular response except that responses are written.

Fishbowl—One or more participants engage in discussion or another activity while others watch and listen.

Trust walk—A blindfolded participant trusts some-one to lead him in some activity.

Responsive reading and singing—The leader reads or sings a passage and others respond vocally.

Skills

Singing, music—Songs and music can greatly enhance family worship. All should participate, but those with musical talent should be encouraged to exercise their gifts in worship.

Drawing, sketching—This may be simple stick figures or works of art, depending upon the ability of family members.

Writing—This may be a written response, a para-phrase, or a more creative effort.

Reading—The "lost art" of oral reading may be recovered in family worship. The Bible lends itself to oral reading and should always be read with feeling and expression.

Paraphrase—Each person puts into his own words, either oral or written, a Bible passage.

Memorization—A verse or passage is best committed to memory only after its meaning is grasped.

Scripture searching—Developing skill in locating books and verses of the Bible is the object of this activity.

Rebus—This is a story told in part with pictures. Children enjoy making and reading these stories.

Crafts—Using common construction materials such as paper, wood, clay, or cloth make objects related to the worship experience.

Refreshments—This is a special treat for children,

particularly when they help to make them. Refreshments may be related to the Bible passage or worship experience.

Storytelling—Children often demonstrate remarkable powers of imagination as they exercise this skill.

Exercises

Clip and paste—Newspapers and magazines may be clipped to make a picture with a special message.

Rank and rate—The idea is to encourage participants to make value judgments or self-examination.

List—This exercise helps organize thoughts, attitudes, impressions.

Test—This is another aid to self-examination.

Chart, graph—This is a graphic device to help clarify thinking.

Fill blanks—Even preschoolers can handle this activity with a little help.

Match—An aid to learning that may also be used as a game.

Recall—A helpful aid in review and follow-up.

Research and report—Schoolchildren are familiar with this one. A good way to settle unanswered questions.

Word association—One word or idea triggers another. This can help parents understand a child's thought processes.

Feelings and Attitudes

Diary—This is an effective method of recording feelings and attitudes.

Gift—Gifts can convey feelings, even if the gift is no more than a thank you.

Goals—A goal can call forth an emotional commitment, particularly if one sets his own goal.

"How I feel"—This requires an honest expression of feelings at the moment.

"What I like/dislike about me"—This activity deals with one's feelings about himself.

"What I like/dislike about others"—Examining personal likes and dislikes and assuming responsibility for them are the goals of this activity.

"What I need"—This activity requires one to examine his needs and desires and what can be done about them.

Scripture reading, discussion, individual and group learning activities, application, prayer, and commitment—these are the elements of family worship. When they are used to involve each member of the family at his own level of understanding, memorable and rewarding experiences in worship result.

3
How to Use
This Guidebook

3
How to Use
This Guidebook

This worship guidebook is addressed to the sponsor and the worship leader. The sponsor is the family member who accepts responsibility for leading the family to become committed to worship in the home. The worship leader guides each worship experience.

Family members should take turns leading worship. Preschoolers may not be capable of leading the entire worship experience, but they can lead in singing a song, quoting a Bible verse, playing a game, and the like. With practice, even preschoolers develop skills in leading worship.

Many youth are highly creative and prefer variety in worship. As youth develop skills and confidence, major responsibility for leading worship may be shifted to them.

The worship leader should study each worship outline in advance. Before the family gathers for worship, the leader should have a worship plan and the necessary materials ready for use. If a child is the worship leader, the sponsor or another older member of the family can help with this preparation.

Experience will soon teach the leader and the sponsor the best time and place for worship in your home. When the family agrees on the best time, this should

be carefully guarded. Of course the time and place
can be changed with changing circumstances. For example, the best time for worship in the summer may
not be the same as when the children are in school.

When the best place for worship is found, materials
for worship may be placed there. This guidebook, Bi-
bles, Bible study aids, paper and pencils, art materials,
and other helps should be available when needed. In-
terrupting worship to look for these materials can jeop-
ardize the entire experience.

When There Are Preschoolers

If the family includes small children, worship must
be adapted to meet their needs. The sponsor and the
worship leader will study each worship outline and
select those elements that seem to have the greatest
appeal for preschoolers and those activities in which
they can participate.

Parents may find such topics as murder and adultery
unsuitable for worship with preschoolers. These outlines may be omitted in favor of other topics more
suitable for children. Small children like familiar stories
and activities. A dozen Bible stories and related activities may be more than enough to meet the worship
needs of preschoolers. Parents can quickly discover the
kinds of materials and activities that get the best response from their children.

If older members of the family need greater depth
and variety in their worship experiences, they may
plan follow-up worship periods. After an initial worship
period with preschoolers, they may be dismissed. Older
members of the family may then engage in worship
on a more mature level.

Adapting the Outlines

The sponsor and the worship leader are the experts in meeting the worship needs of your family. Just as you learn the best time and place for worship in your home, experience will also teach you the kinds of worship experiences that get the best response.

You may find that your family prefers worship that centers around discussion and questions and answers. In that case you will make discussion prominent. On the other hand, your family may like activities rather than talk. This is often the preference of children. Study the worship outlines in advance and select those activities that get the best results with your family.

Occasionally a worship outline may offer little or nothing that seems to fit your family's worship needs. In that case, turn to the chapter, "The How of Family Worship." Study the wide variety of activities listed there, select one that seems to fit your needs, and adapt it to the worship experience.

Where to Go from Here

There are more than fifty-five worship outlines in this guide. Because many of the follow-up activities will require several days to complete, many families will find this material adequate to guide worship experiences for a year.

After all the worship outlines have been followed, the guidebook may be used again. This method is especially effective with small children, who prefer familiar stories and activities repeated many times.

With repeated use, this guidebook should become more helpful. As the worship leader and the sponsor

learn the kinds of experiences that get the best results
in the family, each outline can be adapted for better
results. Suggestions in the outlines may be supple-
mented with those listed in chapter two.

An excellent guide for daily family worship is "The
Family Worships" section of *Home Life* magazine.*
The oral reading in *Home Life* may be combined with
the activities suggested in this guide.

The guide may be combined with outlines for daily
family worship. Daily experiences in worship may be
enriched with learning activities and follow-up activities suggested here.

Perhaps the most effective worship experiences are
those designed by the family to meet their own needs.
On the basis of experience gained from the use of this
guide, the sponsor and the worship leader may select
Bible material, beam it to the worship needs of the
family, and enrich it with the kinds of activities that
get the best response and participation from family
members.

* *Home Life* magazine is a monthly publication of the Family
  Ministry Department of The Baptist Sunday School Board
  of the Southern Baptist Convention.

4
Old Testament
Family Life

4
Old Testament Family Life

Brother Against Brother

Read Genesis 4:1-15. Read the passage responsively, the leader reading the first verse, the family the second, and so on. Talk about the meaning of the passage. Ask: Why was Cain angry? Of what sin was Cain guilty before he murdered Abel (v. 7)? How did Cain answer when God asked about his brother? What was Cain's punishment? Why did he feel that it was more than he could bear?

Invite each member of the family to recall the last time he was very angry. Ask: How did you handle your anger? Why is anger dangerous?

Answer the question, "Am I my brother's keeper?" Talk about ways in which each one is his brother's keeper. List some of the results when we deny responsibility for our brother.

Distribute pages of a daily newspaper to each member of the family. Suggest that each one look for articles, pictures, and other material illustrating how someone acted as his brother's keeper or denied responsibility for his brother. Share your findings.

Point out that today most murders and homicides take place among close acquaintances—family, friends, neighbors, relatives—rather than among strangers or enemies. Can you agree on why this is true?

Talk about the amount of crime and violence shown on television. Ask: What effect does this violence have on families, particularly children? What can families do about this danger? What will our family do?

Pray that God will help you not to be overcome by evil but to overcome evil with good.

In Search of a Bride

Read Genesis 24:1–4,15–21,32–38,50–55,58–67. Because of the length of this passage, you may wish to read the entire chapter in advance and then retell this thrilling story in your own words during family worship.

Talk about the meaning of the passage. Ask: Why did Abraham want his son to have a wife from his own people rather than from the Canaanites? What did Rebekah do that indicated she might make a good wife?

Ask: Does this method of choosing a wife seem unusual? Point out that in many Oriental countries mate selection is done by the parents. Discuss the strengths and weaknesses of this method of selection. Ask: Which method do you prefer, mate selection by parents or by the persons to be married? Why?

Suggest that the husband and wife discuss how they

met. Ask: Where did you meet and when? How long did you know each other before you began to discuss marriage? How did you include your parents in your marriage plans? Did the husband ask the wife's father for her hand in marriage? What were the circumstances?

Ask the husband and wife to recall some of the traits that first attracted them to each other. Ask: Do you still find these traits attractive?

If there are teenagers in the family, invite them to describe what they regard as an ideal courtship.

Draw a picture of the meeting of Isaac and Rebekah, or write an essay describing the thoughts that might have gone through Rebekah's mind as she approached the end of her journey.

Pray that God will direct youth in their search for mates.

A Family Quarrel

Read Genesis 27:1–40. Present this passage as a dramatic reading, the leader reading the narration, another the words of Isaac, another the words of Rebekah, another the words of Jacob, and another the words of Esau. If possible, read from a modern language translation that uses quotation marks.

Talk about the meaning of the passage. Ask: How

did each member of the family contribute to the conflict? Where did the conflict begin? If one member of the family had shown the strength of character, could he have prevented this conflict?

Ask someone who is familiar with the story to summarize briefly what went before and what followed the events in this passage.

Ask: Is it possible for a family to live together without some tension and conflict? Point out that the problem for families is not how to avoid conflict but how to handle it constructively.

Talk about the kinds of situations that sometimes cause tension and conflict in your family. List these areas of conflict. Ask: How do we usually handle these problems? How can we improve the way we deal with conflict?

Re-create a conflict situation in one of the areas you have listed. Talk about how you handled the conflict. Then agree on some ways in which the handling of the situation might have been improved.

Invite each member of the family to make a list of at least three actions he will take to reduce tension and conflict and to build family harmony. Help preschoolers with their lists. Suggest that each one share his list with the family.

Pray for family harmony.

A Suitor Is Tricked

Read Genesis 29:1–20. Read this passage responsively, the leader reading the first verse, the family the second, and so on. Talk about the meaning of the passage.

Ask someone who is familiar with the story to summarize briefly what follows this passage, telling how Laban tricked Jacob.

Ask: How does the relationship between Leah and Rachel illustrate some of the ills of polygamy? What effect did it have on their family life? Why is this practice illegal in the United States?

Ask the wife: When did you first know that your husband loved you? Ask the husband: When did you first know that your wife loved you? Were tokens of love exchanged?

Ask the husband and father to tell about what he has invested of time, money, and energy in support of his wife and family. Ask: What rewards have you received? Suggest that each child thank the father for one provision he has made for which the child is especially grateful.

Suggest that each child prepare a gift for his parents that symbolizes the parents' marriage bonds and the child's appreciation for those bonds. The gift may be a drawing, a poem or essay, or a symbolic token made of paper, cloth, wire, straw, wood, or some other material. The gifts may be displayed in the worship area.

As a prayer, sing the chorus "We Are One in the Spirit."

Joseph and His Brothers

Read Genesis 37:3–28. Discuss the meaning of the passage. Ask: How do you feel toward Jacob? toward Joseph? toward his brothers? Should all the blame for this tragedy be placed on Joseph's brothers, or was the blame shared by Joseph and his father?

Ask someone who knows how this story ends to tell it briefly in his own words.

Ask: Have you ever been jealous or envious of another? How did you handle your feelings?

Read the following story, or retell it in your own words.

Sue was beginning to wonder if anyone loved her. She was only five and had not yet started to school. Her sister Doris was in the second grade and was doing quite well. Doris could already read and write, and her parents were delighted with her progress. They seemed to talk of nothing else but how smart Doris was and how rapidly she was learning. Nothing that Sue did seemed to please her parents nearly so much as her sister's school work.

Talk about Sue's problem. What should her parents

do about it? What should Sue do? How could Doris help? How could the problem have been avoided?

Play a guessing game. Say, I'm thinking of something frightening called "the green-eyed monster." Do you know what it is? Then talk about how to handle this monster, jealousy.

Pray that there may be no partiality or jealousy in your family.

The Ten Commandments

Read Exodus 20:1–17. In advance, assign this passage to a member of the family to study in a Bible commentary and report his findings. If there is a teenager in the family, he may enjoy this assignment. A commentary probably is available in the church library if the family does not have one.

Talk about the meaning of the passage. Note that these Commandments were familiar to Jesus and were quoted by him (refer to Mark 10:19). Point out that these Commandments have stood the test of thousands of years and are the foundation for laws governing human conduct around the world.

Ask: Which Commandments deal with man's relationship to God? Which Commandments deal with man's relationship to his fellowman? Which Commandments apply to family life? Which Commandment do you think is most important? Which is most frequently broken? Which do you find hardest to keep?

Play a matching game. Write the numbers one through ten on a large sheet of paper then read a Commandment and see if the family can match it with the correct number.

After you have discussed the Commandments and the meaning of each one, plan to memorize them. Use the large sheet of paper you used in playing the matching game to study each Commandment. Repeat them aloud together. Next, read a part of each Commandment and let the family complete it. Each one may copy the Commandments for individual study. After you have learned the Commandments, take turns reciting them aloud.

As a prayer, read Psalm 119:11, "Thy word have I hid in mine heart, that I might not sin against thee." Then repeat the verse aloud together.

We Will Serve the Lord

Read Joshua 24:14–25. Before you read the passage, tell the family to listen for a choice that the people of Israel had to make. After the reading, call for responses. Note the number of times the word "serve" appears in the passage.

Joshua called upon the people to put away the

strange or false gods they had served. Talk about some of the false gods families and individuals serve today. Ask: Has our family ever been guilty of serving any of these gods? Are any of these false gods in our house or lives now? What can we do to put them out?

Which god did Joshua and his house choose to serve (v. 15)? Ask: Is our family committed to serving the Lord God? List some ways that your family can declare its allegiance to God. Some suggestions: prayer, Bible study, family worship, church attendance, stewardship, ministry, missions, evangelism, living together in love.

In one home was displayed a plaque: "This house shall be a house of prayer." Ask: Did displaying the plaque make the home a place of prayer? What can make a home a place of prayer?

Plan one action your family will take immediately so that your home may serve God more effectively. Decide how each one will participate in the action.

As a prayer, sing the hymn "God, Give Us Christian Homes."

A Father's Rash Vow

Read Judges 11:29–40. Read this passage responsively, the leader reading the first verse, the family the second, and so on. Talk about the meaning of the passage. Ask: How did Jephthah feel when he returned home and saw his daughter? How did the daughter feel when her father told her what he had done?

In advance, ask someone to read the first part of this chapter and report on the home life of Jephthah and what went before the events in the passage that was read. Ask: Did Jephthah's home life affect the kind of man he became?

William Wordsworth wrote, "The child is father of the man." Can you agree on the meaning of these words?

Ask: Have you ever done or said anything rashly? How did you feel? What did you do about it? How can we avoid rash actions?

Talk about how children sometimes suffer for the mistakes of their parents. Consider how parents also may suffer for the mistakes their children make.

Build a house of cards then have one of the children remove a card and see what happens. Talk about how a family is like that: What happens to one member can affect the entire family.

Suggest that each one make a decorative poster or plaque paying tribute to another member of the family. Examples: "Super Dad" or "To the Greatest Daughter in the World." Display these in the place of worship.

Read Proverbs 3:5–6, "Trust in the Lord with all thine heart; and lean not unto thine own understanding. In all thy ways acknowledge him, and he shall direct thy paths." Talk about what the words mean. Memorize these verses. Then repeat them together as a prayer.

Love Between In-laws

Read Ruth 1:3–18. Present this as a dramatic reading, the leader reading the narration, another the words of Naomi, and another the words of Ruth. Talk about the meaning of the passage. Ask: Are you surprised that the pledge of love and devotion in verses 16–17 was spoken by an in-law rather than by a husband or wife? Why did Ruth feel such strong attachment to her mother-in-law?

Ask someone who is familiar with the story to summarize briefly the book of Ruth.

Invite each one to mention a favorite relative or in-law and tell why that person is a favorite. Ask: What makes that person attractive to you?

Talk about in-laws, especially mothers-in-law and daughters-in-law. Ask: Is our relationship with in-laws like that of Ruth and Naomi? What can we do to strengthen these relationships?

Ask: Why are mothers-in-law often the object of criticism and ridicule? What makes the mother-in-law role especially difficult?

Play a guessing game. Take turns offering a clue to the identity of a relative or in-law as other members of the family try to guess the relative. Keep adding clues until the relative is identified. Example: I am thinking of a relative who is a talented musician.

Plan some action the family will take to strengthen

ties with relatives, such as a letter, call, gift, visit, or the like. Include each member of the family in the project.

Pray for loving ties between relatives such as those that bound Ruth and Naomi.

A Child Given to God

Read 1 Samuel 1;3–28. Read the passage responsively, the leader reading the first verse, the family the second, and so on. Discuss the meaning of the passage. Look up the name *Samuel* in a Bible dictionary. Ask: What vow did Hannah make and how did she keep her vow? Contrast this vow with the rash vow made by Jephthah (Judg. 11:29–40).

Suggest that the parents compare the birth of their children with the birth of Samuel. Ask: Did you ask God for children? Did you dedicate your children to God? How?

Play a guessing game, guessing the identity of children of the Bible. Examples: I was hidden in an ark of bulrushes; who am I? I was born in a manger; who am I? I was the second born of twins; who am I?

Read the following story, or retell it in your own words.

Bill was born to Christian parents who loved each other and their son very much. From his infancy Bill's parents prayed with him and read the Bible to him. They took him to church and taught him about God's love. They tried to show Bill how to live by setting a Christian example for him. Bill learned early that he was loved, wanted, and important.

Dorothy was born in a home not far from Bill's. Her parents did not love each other and were divorced shortly after Dorothy was born. Dorothy's mother did not want her and gave her to an aunt to rear. The aunt was an alcoholic. She was kind to Dorothy when she was sober, but abused her during her frequent drinking bouts. The alcoholic woman's husband resented Dorothy and urged his wife to get rid of the child.

Talk about the difference in the home life of Bill and Dorothy. Ask: How important to a child is a good beginning? Which of these children has the better chance of becoming a well-adjusted adult? Can Dorothy overcome her handicaps? How?

Thank God for the influence of Christian parents and a Christian home.

A Son Is Chosen

Read 1 Samuel 16:1–13. Read this passage responsively, the leader reading the first verse, the family the second, and so on. Talk about the meaning of the passage. Ask: As David was anointed, how did his father feel? his brothers? Samuel? David?

Play a matching game. Copy the data below on a sheet large enough for all the family to see. Then challenge them to correctly match the brothers in the right column with the facts about them in the left column. Verify answers with the help of a Bible dictionary or concordance.

His oldest brother came to his rescue.	Cain and Abel
He murdered his brother.	Jacob and Esau
He told his brother about Jesus	Moses and Aaron
He and his twin brother quarreled.	Joseph and Reuben
He and his brother wanted to sit at Jesus' side.	Andrew and Simon
He was spokeman for his brother.	James and John

Read the following story, or retell it in your own words.

Paul was the youngest of four brothers. His brothers were big and muscular, and all three were outstanding athletes. Paul's parents were proud of their athletic sons. They attended all of the athletic events in which their sons participated and kept notebooks with clippings and pictures of the accomplishments of each one. The living room of their home was filled with trophies that the three boys had won.

Paul was not an athlete. He had neither the interest nor the gifts to excel in sports. He felt inadequate. For solace, he turned to drugs and other kinds of entertainment.

Talk about Paul's problem. Ask: Could it have been avoided? What should Paul have done? How could his family have helped? Is his situation hopeless?

Pray that each member of the family may discover his unique talents and that the family will help each one to develop his talents.

A Father Loses His Son

Read 2 Samuel 18:24–33. Present this as a dramatic reading, the leader reading the narration, another the words of David, another the words of the watchman, and another the words of the runners. Discuss the meaning of the passage. Ask: What factors might have caused the breakdown in the relationship between King David and his son Absalom?

Ask someone who is familiar with the story to summarize briefly what went before and what followed the events in this passage.

Talk about the pressures sometimes felt by the children, particularly the sons, of a famous or successful father. Ask: What can be done to relieve these pressures?

Read the following story, or retell it in your own words.

Mr. Brown was a highly successful lawyer and one of the most influential men in his community. He had

attended a leading university where he was captain
of the football team. Mr. Brown's dream was that his
son, John, would also attend the same university, play
football there, and return home to take over the law
firm he had established.

Tension between Mr. Brown and his son grew as
the boy entered high school and showed no interest
in football or other athletics. Their relationship was
near the breaking point when, in his senior year in
high school, John announced that he was not interested
in law school. He was interested in cars and wanted
to attend a technical school and develop his skills as
an automobile mechanic.

Analyze the conflict between John and his father.
What should they do about it? Is a compromise possible? Could the conflict have been avoided?

Pray for better communication between parents and
children.

The Prophet's Room

Read 2 Kings 4:8–11. Talk about the meaning of the
passage. Ask: How do you think Elisha felt toward the
couple who opened their home to him?

Encourage each one to recall the most unforgettable
visitor you have ever had in the home. Ask: Why was
the visitor unforgettable? What was his most outstand-

ing trait? What impression did he make on your life?

Ask each one to tell about the most memorable home he ever visited. Ask: Why did the home impress you? Would you like to return? Why?

Suggest that each member write a paragraph on the topic, "Impressions I think a visitor would have of our home." Compare the papers and discuss. Lead preschoolers to talk about what they think visitors would notice about your home and write a summary for them.

Plan to invite someone for a meal who has never visited your home—a neighbor, a lost person, a lonely or elderly person, someone of another racial or ethnic group, a shut-in. Decide how each one will help in preparation for the guest.

Memorize Hebrews 13:2, "Be not forgetful to entertain strangers."

Pray that your home may be so filled with love that all who enter may be warmed by it.

Daniel's Training Table

Read Daniel 1:3–20. Read this passage responsively, the leader reading one verse and the rest of the family reading the next. Ask a member of the family to retell the story in his own words.

Talk about the meaning of the passage. Ask: Why was this a difficult decision for Daniel and his friends?

What might have happened had they failed?

Ask members of the family to tell about times when they underwent rigorous training such as military or athletic training, dieting, and the like. What were the results? Did the results justify the training?

Point out that Daniel and his friends felt much pressure to conform to the king's demands. Clip from magazines pictures suggesting worldly pressures today— materialism, pleasure, dissipation, social status, self-indulgence, and the like. Paste these clippings on a flat surface to make a collage. Display the collage in the place of worship. Talk about these pressures and how the family deals with them.

Talk about the temptations to intemperate living and abuse of the body: use of tobacco, alcohol, and other drugs; overeating, overworking, inadequate rest, over-exerting, inactivity. Lead each member of the family to identify those temptations that are most difficult for him to resist.

Urge each member of the family to identify at least one way in which he will seek to build a stronger, healthier body, whether by exercising, dieting, or some other method. Suggest that each one keep a record of his training routine and later share the results with the family.

Thank God for strong bodies and pledge to keep them strong and healthy.

5
The Life
and Teachings of Jesus

5
The Life
and Teachings of Jesus

The Boy Jesus in the Temple

Read Luke 2:41–52. Talk about the meaning of the passage. Ask: What kind of twelve-year-old boy do you think Jesus was? How was he like other boys? In what ways was he different? What is the meaning of verse 51?

Talk about trips the family has taken together. Which trip was the most memorable? Why?

Ask: Have you ever been lost or separated from parents? How did you feel? How did you react when you were reunited with your parents? How was your experience different from that of Jesus?

Play a lost-and-found game. One person says, "I have lost a Bible verse (or Bible character)," then he quotes a part of the verse or tells something about the Bible character. The one who knows the answer says, "I have found it (or him/her)" and completes the Bible verse or identifies the Bible character.

Suggest that the parents recall some experiences they had when they were about twelve years old. How was life different then than it is for twelve-year-olds today? Did the parents have any unusual religious experiences at that age?

Suggest that each one give one reason why he likes being a part of the family.

Thank God for family togetherness.

Jesus and His Brothers

Read John 7:1–9. Talk about the meaning of the passage. Ask: Why do you suppose the Bible records so little about Jesus' home life?

In this passage, Jesus' brothers seem to be chiding or challenging him to show what he can do. They were skeptical of his power and mission. Ask: Would you like to have Jesus for a brother? How would you treat him? After hearing answers, point out that it was difficult for Jesus' brothers not to be jealous of the attention he received or to believe that their brother was different from them.

Read the following fable, or retell it in your own words.

In a farmyard where there were many ducks, one duck was different. This duck, unlike all the other ducks in the farmyard, could fly. Each day he would soar over the farmyard and look down on the earthbound ducks below.

"Why don't you stay on the ground like the rest of us?" the other ducks asked. "Act like a normal farmyard duck, and stop all that silly flying around over us."

At first the duck that could fly paid the others no heed. He continued to fly each day. Soon the other ducks ignored him. They did not include him in their conversations or social gatherings. The duck that could fly became very lonely. At last he quit flying.

After he had remained on the ground for a long while, the duck that once could fly was still lonely. The other ducks ignored him and would not talk to him.

"I have quit flying," the duck said. "Why do you continue to ignore me?"

"Why should we pay you any attention?" said the other ducks. "You are just like the rest of us now."

Talk about the meaning of the fable and the importance of knowing what you want to do in life and doing it, even when those who are close to you are critical.

Pray that God will help each one to praise the special gifts of others and not be critical of them.

Jesus and the Children

Read Mark 10:13–16. Compare this passage with Matthew 19:13–15 and Luke 18:15–17. Also compare the King James Version with a modern language translation.

Talk about the meaning of the passage. Ask: Why do you think the disciples were annoyed that the children were brought to Jesus? Why was Jesus indignant? What do you think Jesus said to the children when he took them up in his arms and blessed them? What do you think Jesus meant when he said the kingdom of heaven must be received like a child?

Play a pretend game. Pretend that you were there when Jesus blessed the children. What would you have said to Jesus? Would you have asked him a question or told him something? Give each one opportunity to respond.

Encourage each child to respond to these questions: Who is your special adult friend outside the family? Why do you like that person? What kind of person is he?

Memorize Mark 10:14. You may prefer to learn the wording in a modern language translation. Talk about the meaning of the words as you memorize them.

Give thanks for a Savior who loves everyone, old and young, adults and children.

Jesus Attends a Wedding

Read John 2:1–11. Present this passage as a dramatic reading, the leader reading the narration; another, the words of Mary; another, the words of Jesus; and a fourth, the words of the steward. This may be more easily read from a modern language translation that uses quotation marks.

Talk about the meaning of the passage. Ask: Do you think it unusual that Jesus performed this first miracle at a wedding? Why did he perform the miracle at a wedding feast rather than in the Temple or while he was preaching?

Talk about weddings the family has attended or participated in. Invite each one to recall the most unusual wedding he ever attended and to tell what made the occasion memorable.

Suggest that parents recall their wedding. Ask: Where was it held? Who attended? How did you feel? Did anything unusual or humorous happen? Do you have any mementos of the wedding to show to the family? Do you have a copy of your marriage license?

If you have a copy of the traditional wedding vows, read them, or recall as many of the words as you can. Discuss the meaning of the vows.

If there are teenagers or single adults in the family, invite them to talk about the kind of wedding they want and why. If they do not plan to marry, invite them to tell why.

Thank God for holy matrimony.

Jesus and Divorce

Read Mark 10:1–12. Compare this passage with Matthew 19:1–9; Genesis 2:24; and Deuteronomy 24:1. Discuss the meaning of the passage. Ask: What did Jesus mean by "the hardness of your heart"?

Point out that America has one of the highest divorce rates in the world. In a recent ten-year period the number of divorces more than doubled, exceeding one million in 1975 for the first time in our history. Ask: What are some factors that contribute to our excessive divorce rate? What actions might be taken by the government, the churches, families, and individuals to reduce the number of divorces?

Think about families you know that have been affected by divorce. Contrast these with other marriages that appear strong and stable. Ask: What made the difference between those marriages that lasted and those that did not?

Study a daily newspaper together. Look for examples of the results of divorce or discord in marriage and family relationships. Do you find any examples of the results of wholesome marriage and family relationships?

Suggest that parents talk about "turning points in our marriage." Ask: Have there been crises in your marriage that strengthened rather than weakened your relationship?

Ask each parent to look the other in the eyes and complete this sentence, "I thank God for you because . . . ."

Hold hands to form a family circle of love. Pray that your love may grow so that the circle may never be broken.

Jesus Visits Friends

Read Luke 10:38–42. Talk about the meaning of the passage. Ask: How do you feel toward Mary? How do you feel toward Martha? Which woman's actions are most like your own?

Ask three members of the family to act out this incident.

Plan how you would entertain Jesus if he should visit in your home. Would you dine out or eat at home? Would you show him the town or stay at home? Would you watch TV or talk? What would you talk about?

Suppose Jesus should visit your home unexpectedly. Would he see or hear anything that might embarrass you? If he should overhear your conversation at mealtime, would he be offended or displeased by anything?

State that Martha allowed household duties to interfere with her time with Jesus. Let each member of the family mention one interest or duty that sometimes crowds out time with Jesus.

Plan one action the family will take to make your home more attractive to Jesus. Some possible actions: greater harmony, sharing of chores, better cooperation, more kindness. Decide how each one will participate.

Pray that the family will become more conscious of the unseen presence of Jesus in your home.

Jesus and the Woman at the Well

Read John 4:5–26. Present this passage as a dramatic reading, the leader reading the narration, a second member of the family the words of Jesus, and a third the words of the woman at the well. Talk about the meaning of the passage. Ask: Why did Jesus reveal himself as the Messiah to this woman of questionable character rather than to the religious leaders?

Compare the conversation of Jesus and the woman at the well with his conversation with Nicodemus as recorded in John 3.

Play a matching game. On a sheet large enough for all the family to see, write the dates in one column and the figures in another, as shown below.

1965	639,000
1969	837,000
1972	1,000,000
1975	479,000

Ask: Can you match the dates with the proper figures which represent the number of divorces in America for that year? When the figures are properly matched, they will show a steady rise in the number of divorces in America from 479,000 in 1965 to more than 1,000,000 in 1975.

Talk about the reasons for the rising divorce rate. Ask: How is increased divorce affecting marriage and family life?

Ask: In light of Jesus' attitude toward the woman who had lived with many husbands, what should be our attitude toward divorced persons? What should be the attitude of the church toward the divorced?

Talk about what your church and community are doing (1) to strengthen marriage, (2) to help the divorced. What more can be done? What can our family do to help?

Pray for stronger, happier marriages.

Anger Between Brothers

Read Matthew 5:21-26. Talk about the meaning of the passage. Compare the King James Version with a modern language translation. Look up the word *raca* in a Bible dictionary or commentary. Ask: Why did Jesus say that the person who is making an offering should first go and be reconciled to his brother?

Play a matching game. Ask members of the family to match the names in the left column with the circumstances in the right column. Study the Scripture references below to verify answers.

Saul   1. Are to not to provoke their children to anger.

Samson   2. In anger he hacked a yoke of oxen in pieces.

David   3. Because his riddle was solved, he killed thirty men.

Haman   4. He was angry because of the hardness of men's hearts.

Jesus   5. In anger he plotted a hanging.

Fathers   6. He was angry because of a prophet's story.

(1 Sam. 11:6-7; Judg. 14:19; 2 Sam. 12:5; Eph. 6:4; Esther 3:5; Mark 3:5)

Invite each one to recall a time when he became angry and lost his temper. Ask: How did you feel afterward? What did you do about it?

Ask: Are you surprised that Jesus showed anger? Talk about the difference between righteous indignation and blind anger. Read Ephesians 4:26. Talk about how one may be angry without sinning.

After discussing the meaning of the verse, memorize Psalm 133:1, "Behold, how good and how pleasant it is for brethren to dwell together in unity!"

Pray that God will help each member of the family to be slow to anger.

A Mother and Her Sons

Read Matthew 20:20–28. You may present this as a dramatic reading, the leader reading the words of Jesus, another the words of the mother, and another the words of the brothers.

Talk about the meaning of the passage. Ask: How do you feel toward the mother? How do you feel toward the brothers? What do you think of the reaction of the disciples? Why do you think Jesus answered as he did? How did the disciples feel after Jesus answered?

Read the following story, or retell it in your own words.

Two Christian parents had two sons of whom they were very proud. One of the boys felt the call of God to the ministry. He attended a seminary where he had an outstanding record. He was called to one influential church after another. Finally he became pastor of one of the largest and most influential churches in his denomination. He preached to a congregation of more than a thousand each Sunday and baptized hundreds of converts each year. He was one of the most honored and respected pastors in the country.

The other son did not attend college or a seminary. He felt called to minister to confused and bewildered youth and young adults. He enlisted the support of churches in the community and established a coffee house. There he ministered to alcoholics, drug addicts, runaways, and derelicts. Because he had little income, he lived in the coffee house and ate and slept with those to whom he ministered. Only a few persons in the community knew about his ministry.

Discuss the story. Ask: Were the parents more proud of one son than the other? Why? Did one son serve more faithfully than the other? Do you believe one son was more pleasing to God than the other? Why?

Pray for willingness to serve wherever God calls.

A Father and His Sons

Read Matthew 21:28–32. Read the passage responsively, the leader reading the words of Jesus and the rest of the family responding by reading the other words. This may be done more easily by using a modern language translation that uses quotation marks or a Bible with the words of Jesus in red. Discuss the meaning of the passage.

Invite members of the family to recall times when

they did something wrong or made a mistake and had to correct their error. Ask: Why is it hard to admit that we are wrong or have made a mistake?

Ask: Which of the sons was disobedient? Talk about disobedience in the family. Point out that disobedience of family authority may lead to disobeying civil authority and even to disobedience toward God. This is one reason God has commanded children to obey their parents. Ask: Who can quote the Fifth Commandment (Ex. 20:12)? Then repeat it together.

Suggest that each one draw a picture or tell a story about the principle of obedience. The picture or story may depict obedience in the home or community or obedience toward God. Display the pictures and stories in the place of worship as a reminder of the need for obedience.

Repeat together as a prayer, "Behold, to obey is better than sacrifice" (1 Sam. 15:22).

Ahead of Family

Read Luke 14:25–33. Compare this passage with Matthew 10:34–39. Talk about the meaning of the passage. Ask: Did Jesus mean that we are to hate the members of our family? Compare Luke 14:26 with Matthew 10:37. Point out that no one who made provision for his mother as he was dying on a cross would teach that we are to hate our family.

Copy the following list on a sheet of paper large enough for all the family to see.

home and family
school or work
church
God
possessions
self
friends and neighbors

Now ask each family member to rearrange the list in the order in which these have priority in his life, from first to last. Talk about the list each one has made. The order of priority probably will not be the same for all. Can you agree that in a well ordered life God should be first and possessions last on this list?

Invite each one to recall something that he wanted very much and what he had to give up or what sacrifices he had to make in order to get what he wanted. Ask: Was the possession worth the sacrifice you had to make?

Talk about the cost of discipleship and some of the sacrifices we may be called upon to make in order to follow Jesus.

As a prayer, sing the hymn "I Surrender All."

A Widow's Offering

Read Mark 12:41–44. Enlist two members of the family to dramatize this incident. Compare this passage with Luke 21:1–4. Talk about the meaning of the passage. Ask: Why did Jesus say that the widow gave more than all the others? Does this suggest that what we keep for ourselves may be as important a part of stewardship as what we give?

Tell the following true story.

A minister in Missouri reversed the usual procedure in his church one Sunday. Instead of receiving an offering, he distributed one thousand dollars to members of the congregation. The church members were instructed to take the money and use it to bring more money back to the church.

There followed a wave of bake sales, lawn–mowing projects, community dinners, music lessons, and other activities designed to increase the amount of money taken from the offering plate. When the day of accounting came, the church members returned more than $3,000 to the church.

"Some people thought the project was about money," the pastor said afterward, "but it was about how we should dedicate our talents to the Lord. The emphasis was upon how we are accountable for all that we receive."

Talk about what the pastor did and how the church members responded. Suggest that the family undertake a similar project. Give to each one a small amount of money, and instruct him to use his own talents or abilities to increase the sum. At the end of an agreed-upon period, let each one give his earnings to the church as an offering.

Thank God for his blessings and pray that each one may be a cheerful giver in return.

Giving Good Gifts

Read Matthew 7:7–11. Read the passage responsively, the leader reading the first verse and the family responding by reading the second, and so on. Compare this passage with Luke 11:9–13. Note the number of times the verbs *ask* and *give* appear in the Matthew passage. Discuss the meaning of the passage.

Point out that a part of this passage may be summarized under an acrostic beginning with the letters *A-S-K*. See who can find it by searching the first part of the passage. Then spell out the acrostic:

A-sk
S-eek
K-nock

Suggest that each one recall a time when he asked God for something and how his prayer was answered.

Talk about unusual blessings that the family has received from God. Ask: What is God's greatest gift? (his Son).

Encourage each one of the children to mention one thing his parents or family have provided for him for which he is especially grateful.

Play a guessing game. Suggest that parents describe a blessing and the children guess what the blessing is. Examples: Without this blessing, you would be cold in winter (warm clothing). This blessing keeps you dry when it rains (a house).

Have sentence prayers, each one thanking God for a particular blessing.

A Blind Man Sees

Read Luke 18:35-43. Before you read, divide the family into two listening teams. Have one team listen for what the blind man said and the other listen for what Jesus said. Hear the reports and discuss them. Compare this passage with Matthew 20:29-34 and Mark 10:46-52. Talk about the meaning of the passage. Ask: How do you think the blind man felt when he received his sight?

Say: Many believe that blindness is the most terrifying of all physical handicaps. Do you agree? Why?

Invite discussion about sightless persons known by members of the family. Discuss their achievements in spite of their handicap. Talk about how they have developed other senses to compensate for their blindness.

Divide into pairs and take "trust walks." One person will close his eyes and let the other lead him about the house or outdoors. Then reverse roles so that each one is led about while his eyes are closed. Talk about the experience. Ask: How did it feel to be sightless and to let someone lead you around?

Say: Jesus once spoke of those who have eyes to see but see not (Mark 8:18). What did he mean? Talk about how we often fail to see and appreciate the marvelous world we live in. Ask: What is spiritual blindness? Talk about how the family may become more aware of the truth of the gospel.

Sing as a prayer "Open My Eyes that I May See."

A Daughter Is Healed

Read Matthew 15:21–28. Before you read, form two listening teams, one to listen for what the woman said and the other to listen for what Jesus said. Hear the reports and discuss them. Compare this passage with Mark 7:24–30. Also compare with the Scripture passages under the topic "A Son Is Healed."

Note especially the unusual words of Jesus in verse 26. Why did Jesus use this language? If you are not certain about the meaning of this passage, assign it to someone to study in a Bible commentary and report his findings.

Invite each member of the family to talk about a time when he was seriously ill and how he was healed. Ask: Did prayer play a part in the healing?

Talk about the change in the status of women from the time of Jesus, when women were regarded as inferior, until today. List some milestones in women's progress, such as Jesus' elevation of women, women's suffrage, equal employment opportunities, and the like.

List some of women's unique qualities and abilities and some of their major contributions to society.

Have an informal debate on this statement: *Resolved,* that a woman should be elected president of the United States.

Suggest that mother and daughters each write an essay on the subject "Why I Thank God That I Am a Woman." Father and sons may write on "Why I Thank God for My Mother (or sisters)."

Thank God for creating men and women as equals.

A Rich Young Man

Read Mark 10:17–22. Compare with Matthew 19:16–30 and Luke 18:18–30. Talk about the meaning of the passage. Ask: Have we kept the Commandments as well as this young man? Why did Jesus tell the man to sell all that he had and give the money to the poor? Why did Jesus love the man?

Discuss the following questions.

What one possession means the most to you? If the house caught on fire and you had time to save only one possession, what would it be?

If you were marooned on a desert island, what one convenience would you miss most? Why?

If you had one thousand dollars to spend in any way that you wished, how would you use it?

Talk about the family's standard of living as compared with that of your neighbors and friends. Then compare your standard of living with that of other families around the world. Try to face this question honestly: If Jesus asked us to give up all our possessions in order to follow him, would we turn away as the young man did?

Discuss the principle of loving people and using things as opposed to loving things and using people.

Agree on one sacrifice the family will make in order to demonstrate your love for the kingdom of God rather than for the things of the world. Plan how each one will participate.

As a prayer, sing the chorus "Turn Your Eyes upon Jesus."

A Little Man Stands Tall

Read Luke 19:1–10. Ask each member of the family to tell what the passage means to him. Some questions you may discuss: How do you think Zacchaeus acquired his wealth? Do you think he was well liked by his fellow townsmen? With all his wealth, was there something Zacchaeus could not buy? Do you think Zacchaeus was happy? What do you think made him want to give back the money he had taken? What did Jesus give to Zacchaeus that was more important than money or height?

Let two members of the family present a skit, one playing the part of Zacchaeus and the other the part of Jesus.

If one of the children has learned a song about Zacchaeus at church, let him teach the song to the family.

Play a game of pretend. Pretend you are Zacchaeus. What is life like for a short man? What are the disadvantages of being short? Are there any advantages? Encourage the children to talk about what it is like to live in a world of bigger, taller adults where chairs, tables, doors, cars, and other objects are made to accommodate adults.

Lead the family to talk about physical appearance. Ask: What do you like or dislike about your body? What would you change about it if you could and why? Talk about attractive or outstanding physical features of each member of the family.

Talk about ways in which we can use our bodies to please God (use our eyes to read the Bible, our lips to tell others about Jesus, our hands to help those in need). Encourage each member of the family to determine at least one way in which he will seek to please God with his body this week.

Pray that each member of the family will be aware that his body is the temple of the Holy Spirit.

A Log in the Eye

Read Matthew 7:1–5. If you read from the King James Version, compare this with a modern language translation. Note the modern language translation for "mote" and "beam." Discuss the meaning of the passage.

Invite each member of the family to talk about some trait or habit for which he is frequently criticized, either by family members or others. Ask: How do you feel about this criticism? Do you believe it is justified? Do you believe you have been judged harshly or unfairly? What have you done about the criticism?

Suggest that each one respond to the following questions.

Do I criticize or pass judgment on others? —— Usually —— Sometimes —— Rarely

Do I always judge others as I would want to be judged? —— Usually —— Sometimes —— Rarely

Before I criticize others, do I first examine my own life to see if I am guilty of the same fault? —— Usually —— Sometimes —— Rarely

Say: Students of human behavior have noted that we often are most critical of the traits or behavior in others that we most dislike in ourselves. Ask: Do you agree? If yes, why do you agree?

Suggest that each one complete the sentence, "The quality that I most dislike about myself is . . . ." Volunteers may share their statements with the family.

On the basis of this experience together, talk about how critical the family is of its members and others. Plan appropriate action on the basis of your conclusions.

Pray together the Lord's Model Prayer (Matt. 6:9–13).

Help for a Widow

Read Luke 18:1–8. Read this passage in unison, each reading from his own Bible. Compare this passage with

Luke 11:5–10. Talk about the meaning of the passage. Ask: Why did Jesus urge us to be persistent in our prayers?

Ask: What is the longest you have ever prayed for a single object of prayer? How was the prayer answered?

Suggest that each one keep a prayer record or diary. Record the object of each prayer, when you began praying for the object, when the prayer was answered, and how. Ask: Do you remember to thank God when your prayers are answered?

Lead a Scripture completion exercise. Read the part of the verse below and see if anyone can complete it. Verify the answer by looking up the reference and reading the verse.

"I caused the widow's heart to _____" (Job 29:13).

"Learn to do well; seek judgment, relieve the oppressed, judge the fatherless, _____ the widow" (Isa. 1:17).

"There came a certain poor widow, and she threw in _____" (Mark 12:42).

"She was a widow of about fourscore and four years, which departed not _____" (Luke 2:37).

"Let not a widow be taken into the number under _____" (1 Tim. 5:9).

Talk about some of the problems of widows (loneliness, finances, illness, no one to perform chores usually done by a man). Ask: What can our family do to help widows?

Plan some action the family will take to aid a widow. Include each one in the project.

Pray for widows and the fatherless.

Choosing a Mate

Read 1 Corinthians 7:1–16. Read this passage from a modern language translation.

Lead a Scripture searching exercise. Give the following references one at a time and call on the first one who finds the reference to read the passage: Mark 10:2–9; 2 Corinthians 6:14–18; 1 Corinthians 7:25–40; 1 Peter 3:1–2. Compare these passages with 1 Corinthians 7:1–16. Talk about the meaning of these passages.

Point out that fewer young adults, particularly women, are choosing to marry today. List some factors that may influence the decision to remain single. Ask: What are the advantages and disadvantages of single adulthood? Why did Paul say that it is better for some Christians to remain single?

Ask the parents to recall where they met and how they became acquainted. Talk about places where one is likely to find a Christian mate (church, homes of friends and relatives) and places where one is less likely to find such a mate (bars, night clubs).

Ask: Why is it wise to date persons with backgrounds, interests, and religious beliefs similar to one's own? What often happens when a Christian marries an unbeliever? When a Christian marries a person of another faith? When Christians marry who have differing doctrinal beliefs?

Suggest that each person list five to ten qualities that

he would expect to find in his ideal mate. Then have each one rate himself on a scale of one to ten on each quality he had listed. Ask: What part do religious beliefs play in your estimation of the ideal mate?

Point out that many single adults and formerly married persons are hungry for family fellowship. Plan to invite one of these adults into your home. Include all the family in the planning and preparation.

Thank God that your home is united in Christian faith.

When a Brother Falls

Read Galatians 6:1–5. Talk about the meaning of the passage. Ask: Why is there no contradiction between verses two and five?

Lead a Scripture searching exercise. Give the following references one at a time, and call on the first one to find the reference to read the passage: 2 Thessalonians 3:14–15; James 5:19–20; Luke 18:9–14; Proverbs 16:18.

Point out that Jesus often warned his disciples against pride and self-righteousness. Ask: Why did Jesus regard these sins as especially dangerous?

Suggest that each one recall a time when he made a mistake or was in error. Ask: Were others critical or helpful? How did this make you feel? When others make a mistake, do you usually point out their error and criticize or try to reassure them?

Read the following story, or retell it in your own words.

Frank, a junior high student, was complaining to his parents about the behavior of some of his friends.

"I try to get them to go to church with me every Sunday," Frank said, "but usually they don't want to go. About the only time they're interested in church is when we are planning a picnic. And they never go visiting with our class. I bet they never study their lessons or read the Bible and pray like I do. And at school they hang around with some of the guys who smoke and tell dirty jokes. You'll never hear me talking like that! And I'll bet I'm the only boy at school that keeps a Bible in his locker."

Talk about Frank's problem. Ask: While Frank's friends seem to have their sins, does Frank also have his? Could Frank be one of the reasons his friends are not more interested in attending church with him? How could Frank make his witness more appealing?

Memorize Proverbs 16:18, "Pride goeth before destruction, and an haughty spirit before a fall."

Ask God to keep you from the sins of pride and self-righteousness.

The Lord's Supper

Read Matthew 26:26–29. Compare this passage with Mark 14:22–25; Luke 22:17–20; and 1 Corinthians 11:23–25. Ask each member of the family to tell what these verses mean to him.

Ask: What do you think Jesus was trying to say to his disciples? Do you think they understood him? How do you think Jesus felt? How do you think the disciples felt? Why did Jesus use a mealtime to do this? Was it only because the bread and the cup were on the table, or was there some other reason?

If there is a reproduction of da Vinci's *The Last Supper* in your home, study it together. If you do not have a reproduction, perhaps the painting is so familiar to the family that you can discuss it. Do you think this is a good portrayal of the scene as it might have happened? What do you like and dislike about the artist's portrayal?

Talk about the observance of the Lord's Supper in your church. Invite each member of the family to share what this experience means to him. Encourage each one to tell how he feels during this observance.

This is a good opportunity to explain to small children why the observance of the Lord's Supper is reserved for those who have made an open commitment of their lives to Jesus.

You may wish to serve light refreshments as a part of this worship experience. Invite the children to have a part in preparing and serving the refreshments.

Give thanks for a loving Savior who gave his life for each member of the family and for all who will receive him.

6
The Royal Law
of Family Life

6
The Royal Law of Family Life

God Is Love

Read 1 John 4:7–8. Before you read the passage, say that you are going to play a listening game. Tell members to listen and count the number of times the word *love* is used. Ask each one to tell what the passage means to him.

Talk about current distortions or misconceptions of love as these are sometimes presented in movies, television, novels, the entertainment world, and elsewhere. Decide what is wrong with these portrayals of love.

Ask: Have you ever made statements like these: "I love ice cream. I love my new dress"? What is wrong with these statements?

Try to agree on a definition of love. First you may talk about what love is not: not lust or passion or mere fondness. Then decide what love is. Refer to 1 Corinthians 13 for help.

Ask: How does God show his love for us? What was God's greatest expression of his love for us?

Encourage each member of the family to tell "one way that God has shown his love for me" or "one way that God is showing his love for me."

Thank God for his boundless love.

We Love Him

Read 1 John 4:15–19. Suggest that each member of the family follow the reading in his own Bible and underline the word *love* each time it appears. You may prefer to read the passage aloud together. Talk about what the words mean.

Encourage each member of the family to name one person whom he loves. After each one has named someone he loves, ask: Why do you love that person? After each one has answered the question, talk about how we often love those who show love toward us or who respond to our love.

Talk about how God first loved us—but not because we were lovable or worthy of his love or even responded to his love. God loved us even when we were sinners who had rejected his love.

Ask: Have you ever tried to love someone who spurned your love or made it clear that he did not return your love? How did it make you feel?

Talk about ways that members of the family can express their love for God: prayer, worship, reading his Word, seeking his will. Note that one of the best ways to show love for God is to love others.

Encourage each one to find some way of expressing his love to God this week.

Memorize verse 19.

Sing as a prayer the first stanza of the hymn "O Love That Wilt Not Let Me Go."

Husbands, Love Your Wives

Read Ephesians 5:25–33. Compare this passage with Colossians 3:19. Talk about the meaning of the passages. The husband may read these passages and lead the discussion of their meaning, especially as he understands them.

Encourage the children to talk about ways their father shows his love for their mother. Discuss the different ways that a husband may show love for his wife: kindness, tenderness, thoughtfulness, care, protection, gifts, words of endearment, caresses.

Ask the wife to recall some of the most meaningful expressions of love that she has received from her husband and why they were most meaningful.

Ask the husband to look at his wife and complete this sentence, "When I was courting you, I knew that I wanted you for my wife when . . . ."

Suggest that the husband tell his wife some of the reasons why he loves her. Encourage him to be specific.

Ask the husband to lead in a prayer of thanks for his wife.

Wives, Love Your Husbands

Read Colossians 3:18 and Titus 2:14. Talk about the meaning of the verses. Ask the wife to read the passages and to lead the discussion of their meaning, especially what the verses mean to her.

Ask the children to talk about ways that their mother shows that she loves their father. Talk about the different ways that a wife may show her love for her husband. Refer to Proverbs 31:10–31.

Ask the husband to tell of some of the most meaningful expressions of love that he has received from his wife and why these expressions of love meant much to him.

Ask the wife to look at her husband and complete this sentence, "When you were courting me, I knew that I wanted you for my husband when. . . ."

Ask the wife to tell about times in their marriage when she has felt closest to her husband and why she felt that way.

Encourage the wife to list some reasons why she loves her husband. Urge her to be specific.

Suggest that the wife lead a prayer of thanksgiving for her husband.

Parents, Love Your Children

Read Ephesians 6:4; Colossians 3:21; and Psalm 127:3–5. Have parents share the reading of these passages and lead a discussion of their meaning.

Ask the mother to recall the birth of each child. Emphasize any unusual or humorous circumstances. Talk about how each baby was different. Father may help recall details.

Ask each parent to identify a quality in each child that the parent especially loves and admires.

Suggest that each parent pledge to express his love for each child in one specific way and to be alert for other ways to show his love. Parents may go to the child and touch him as they do this.

If a child is absent, plan a special expression of love for the absent member, such as a letter, gift, telephone call, or a package from home. Encourage each one to contribute to this expression of love.

Ask parents to lead in a joint prayer of thanksgiving for their children.

Children, Love Your Parents

Read Ephesians 6:1–3 and Colossians 3:20. Ask a child to read the passages. Talk about the meaning of the passages. Ask the children to put into their own words what the verses mean to them.

Encourage each child to tell of one way that his parents show their love for him that is especially meaningful to him and to tell why that expression of love means much to him.

Suggest that each child do something to show his love for his parents. Encourage each child to exercise his own talents in showing his love. This may be to write a letter or poem, prepare a favorite dish, offer to do chores, draw a picture, knit or crochet a gift, or make a knickknack.

Encourage each child to pledge to show his love for his parents in other ways during the week.

Thank God for parents who love sacrificially for their children.

Love One Another

Read John 15:9–12. Ask each member of the family to follow the reading in his Bible. Each time the word *love* appears in the passage, all will read this word aloud. Talk about the meaning of the passage. Ask: What does it mean to love others as Jesus loved us?

Encourage each member of the family to tell "why my family is special to me."

Place a chair in the center of the family circle. Ask each member of the family in turn to sit in the chair. As each one takes his place in the chair, other members of the family will tell about one quality or trait of the one in the chair that he especially loves and admires.

Talk about ways that love for one another in the family can be strengthened. Encourage each one to plan one action that he will take to strengthen family love.

In advance, clip from a magazine a picture of a family group. Cut the picture into small pieces like a jigsaw puzzle. Put all of the pieces of the puzzle except one on the table, and ask the family to put the puzzle together. When the puzzle is complete except for one piece, say: That is what our family is like when one is absent.

If a member of the family is absent (in school, in military service, married, moved away, ill or hospitalized), plan some special way that the family will show love for the absent member. Decide how each one will participate.

Have sentence prayers, letting each one thank God in his own way for his family.

Love Your Neighbor

Read Luke 10:25–37. Act out this familiar story of the good Samaritan. Family members may have to play more than one part. Talk about the meaning of the passage. Ask: Why do you think Jesus answered the lawyer in this way?

Discuss examples of good neighbors that members of the family have observed. Ask: Who is the best neighbor you have ever known? Have you told that person how you feel about him?

Recall times when others showed neighborliness to the family or a member of the family.

Make a list of persons you know who are especially in need of good neighbors (aged, disadvantaged, shut-ins, minority groups, handicapped persons, prisoners, sick and hospitalized, strangers and displaced persons, military personnel, drug addicts, alcoholics, social outcasts).

Discuss ways that the family can show neighborliness. Rate yourself on how neighborly you think your family is. List your strengths and weaknesses as good neighbors.

Plan one specific action the family will take to show neighborliness to someone in the group mentioned above. Decide how each one will participate.

Pray that you may grow in neighborliness.

Love the Brethren

Play a Scripture searching game. Call out the following Scripture references one at a time, and let the first one who finds each reference read the passage: 1 Peter 3:8; Ephesians 5:1–2; 1 Peter 2:17; 1 John 3:14–17.

Talk about the meaning of the verses. Ask: Is it possible to love in word but not in deed? Talk about the meaning of the statement, "Love is something you do."

Encourage each member of the family who is a Christian to recall his baptism and his first observance of the Lord's Supper.

Ask each one to tell about one aspect of church life that is especially enjoyable to him and why.

Invite each one to tell how the church or some member of the church has ministered or shown love to him.

Talk about ways the family can strengthen the life and work of the church (prayer, attendance, giving, serving).

Plan one action the family will take to strengthen home-church ties and the life of the church. Decide how each one will take part in the action.

Sing as a prayer the hymn "I Love Thy Kingdom, Lord."

Love Your Enemies

Read Matthew 5:43–48. Talk about the meaning of the passage. Some say that this is one of Jesus' hardest teachings. Ask: Do you agree? Why?

Encourage each member of the family to recall a recent quarrel or conflict in which he was involved and how it was resolved.

Ask: What is the best demonstration of this teaching of Jesus that you have ever observed? Invite each member of the family to respond.

Ask: Can you think of a time when a member of the family practiced this teaching? Discuss responses.

Read and discuss Matthew 5:9. Talk about how members of the family can be peacemakers—in the home, the neighborhood, the school, the shop and office, the community, the world.

Plan one specific peacemaking action the family will take, such as seeking to reconcile two persons who are at odds or engaging in some activity to discourage war and promote peace. Encourage everyone to participate.

Read as a prayer Isaiah 2:2–5.

The Greatest Gift Is Love

Read 1 Corinthians 13. Use a modern language translation that translates *charity* as *love*. Read the passage responsively, the leader reading the first verse, the family reading the second, and so on. Talk about the meaning of the passage.

Underscore or count the number of times the word "love" appears in the passage. Try to define love.

Distribute paper and pencils and instruct family members to make two lists. (Preschoolers may work with older members or draw a picture of someone showing love.) The family will study the passage together. Then each one will make one list outlining what love is and a second list of what love is not. Compare the completed lists with your definition of love.

Suggest that each family member study his lists and rate himself on a scale of one to ten on each point. Each one should ask himself: On what points do I need to show greater love?

Following the individual rating, lead the family to rate itself as a group on the same points. Talk about family strengths and weaknesses in showing love for one another.

Select one or more points on which the family is weak in showing love. Plan actions the family will take to overcome these weaknesses. Decide how each one will participate.

As a prayer, sing the chorus "For God So Loved the World."

7
For Holidays
and Special Occasions

7
For Holidays
and Special Occasions

New Year's Day

Read Genesis 32:24–28. Enlist three readers to read this passage, one to read the narration, another to read the words of Jacob, and a third to read the words of the angel. If possible, read from a modern language translation that uses quotation marks. Discuss the passage.

In advance, ask a family member to look up in a Bible dictionary or other Bible study aid the meaning of the names *Jacob* and *Israel* and to bring a report at family worship. Discuss the reason for this change of names.

Enlist another family member to research in an encyclopedia or other resource book and report at family worship on the Roman god Janus, from which our word *January* comes. Display a picture of this god with opposite faces. Discuss the appropriateness of this figure, which looks both forward and backward, in representing the new year or a new beginning.

Look backward over the year just ended. Recall some of its highlights for your family. What blessings were received? What prayers were answered? What crises did God see you through?

Look forward to the year ahead. What goals should the family set? How can you strengthen your family life? How can you achieve greater spiritual growth than you did during the year just ended? How can you demonstrate greater faithfulness in discipleship? Write out these goals and post them in the place of worship as a reminder.

Talk about ways of celebrating the new year. Contrast the drunken revelry of some with the watch night prayer services of others. Ask: How should a Christian mark the arrival of a new year?

Recall the most meaningful New Year's Day you ever experienced. What made that occasion special?

Encourage each one to recall a time when he made a fresh start—in school, in business, in his religious pilgrimage, or some other time. Ask: What did this experience mean to you?

Thank God for the new year with all its opportunities. Pray that each member of the family may use each day wisely. Close the prayer by repeating together, "So teach us to number our days, that we may apply our hearts unto wisdom" (Ps. 90:12).

Easter

Read Matthew 28:1–8. Enlist two readers for this passage, one to read the narration and the other to read the words of the angel.

Ask a family member to be prepared to tell in his own words about the last hours of Jesus on earth from the time he observed the last Supper with the disciples until his resurrection. Talk about why these have been called the most crucial hours in the history of mankind.

Informally debate the question of whether Christmas or Easter is the most important date on the Christian calendar. Conclude the discussion by emphasizing the importance of both the birth and the resurrection of Jesus.

Talk about ways in which Easter has been made unchristian by practices that have no bearing on the true meaning of this holy day. Compare these practices with similar practices surrounding Christmas and other holy days, including Sunday.

Ask: What is our family doing to observe the true spirit of Easter? What more can we do to emphasize the significance of this special day?

Plan some project the family will carry out during the Easter season, such as minister to a widow or orphans or a bereaved family, decorate a grave or clean up an abandoned cemetery, contribute to a special Easter offering, or give a gift in memory of a deceased person.

Read 1 Corinthians 15:51–57. Talk about the resurrection Jesus made possible for all who believe in him. Pray that Easter may bring to each member of the family a renewed sense of commitment to the risen Lord.

Mother's Day

Read John 19:23–27. Ask another to read Psalm 22:1,14–18. Talk about the meaning of the passage.

Ask: How do you think the disciple felt when Jesus said this? How did Jesus' mother feel? How do you feel toward Jesus for suggesting this?

Talk about unusual mothers of the Bible and of history. Ask: Which of these mothers is your favorite and why?

Suggest that each child go to Mother, embrace her, and say, "Mother, I love you because . . . ," completing the sentence with one special reason why he loves his mother.

Suggest that each child plan some special way that he will show his love for his mother during the next few days. This may be a gift, an act of kindness or helpfulness, or some other surprise expression of love.

Parents and other adults in the family whose mothers are still living may also plan some special surprise expression of love for their mothers.

Read Proverbs 31:10–31.

Thank God for Christian mothers and their influence.

Father's Day

Read Genesis 22:1–14. Talk about the meaning of this unusual passage. Ask: What thoughts went through the mind of Abraham as he made his way to the place of sacrifice? What did Isaac think as he finally realized what was about to happen? Do you think Isaac was suspicious when he asked about the lamb for sacrifice?

Ask: Do you know of a father who did sacrifice his

son? Why did God sacrifice his only Son? What does this sacrifice mean to you?

Play a matching game. Match the biblical fathers in the left column with their sons in the right column. Copy the lists on paper large enough for all the family to see. To verify your answers, look up the names in a Bible concordance or dictionary.

Adam	Joseph
Jacob	Absalom
David	Abel
Nun	Joshua
Isaac	David
Kish	Esau
Jesse	Saul

Evaluate each of the above father-son relationships: good, bad, or unknown.

Suggest that the parents talk about "what I remember about my father." List several of his outstanding traits.

Invite each child to complete this sentence: "I love my father because . . . ."

Plan some special expression of love and appreciation for Father. Include all members of the family in the planning and preparation.

Thank God for fathers who honor God.

July Fourth

Read Matthew 22:15–22. Enlist three readers for this passage, one to read the narration, another to read the words of the Pharisees, and a third to read the words of Jesus.

In advance, enlist a family member to research and report at family worship on the part evangelical Christians played in establishing religious freedom in America. The church librarian may help in this project.

Using an encyclopedia or other resource book, read the First Amendment to the Constitution. Talk about the importance of this amendment for religious freedom.

Invite each member of the family to tell about at least one of his favorite things about the Fourth of July.

Ask older children or youth to give a brief talk or write an essay on "Why I Am Thankful to Be an American." Younger children may draw a picture showing what they like about living in America.

Conduct a family quiz on "Facts About Our Country," letting each one in turn ask a question and see if others can answer it. Sample questions: How many men have served as president of the United States? Which president served longest? When was the Declaration of Independence signed? How many amendments have been made to the Constitution? Which state is the smallest? The largest? Who discovered America? When?

Sing "America the Beautiful."

Have sentence prayers, each member of the family naming one thing about his country for which he is especially thankful.

Thanksgiving

Read Psalm 100 in unison. Talk about the meaning of this passage then memorize the psalm together.

Enlist a family member to look up the origin of Thanksgiving in an encyclopedia or other resource book and to bring a report to family worship. Talk about why this holiday is special for Americans.

Instead of the report on the origin of Thanksgiving, or perhaps following this report, present a skit on the first Thanksgiving. Make the skit as simple or as elaborate as you wish, but include the children in the planning and acting.

Ask each member of the family to pretend that he is present at the first Thanksgiving. Ask: What are you thankful for? What are you thankful for today?

Play a guessing game using symbols associated with Thanksgiving. Example: I am thinking of a symbol for Thanksgiving that makes a strange "gobble, gobble" sound. Others: family reunion, football game, harvesttime, day at home.

In advance, cut from a magazine a colorful picture representative of Thanksgiving then cut the picture into parts to make a jigsaw puzzle. Let the family put the puzzle together.

Invite each person to suggest blessings for which the family is especially thankful today. Join hands and ask someone to lead in a prayer of thanksgiving.

Christmas

Read Matthew 1:18–24. Compare this passage with Luke 1:26–38 and Isaiah 7:14. Talk about the meaning of the passage. Ask: What thoughts do you suppose were going through Mary's and Joseph's minds at this time?

Suggest that each one recall the happiest Christmas he ever experienced. Ask: What made that Christmas memorable?

Talk about what each person likes best about Christmas and why—carols, worship, gifts, food, reunions, decorations, surprises, Christmas morning.

Ask: Does our family have a special family tradition or ritual at Christmas? Talk about the ritual and why you have continued it. If you do not have a special family tradition, you may wish to begin one.

Try to define the true spirit of Christmas. List some of the elements of the true Christmas spirit, such as love, joy, peace, unselfishness.

Say: Christmas is the highlight of the entire Christian calendar, the most joyous time of the year. Yet studies show that for many persons this is a sad and lonely time. Drinking, accidents, homicides, and suicides increase at this time. Ask: Why is this a sad and lonely time for many? Do we know any of these persons? What can we do to help them?

Plan some activity that you believe expresses the

true spirit of Christmas. Be sure to include each member of the family in your planning.

As a prayer, sing a favorite Christmas carol.

Birth

Read Exodus 2:1–10. During or following the reading, present this scene as a skit, one member of the family playing the part of Pharaoh's daughter and another the part of Moses' sister. A child's doll may represent the baby Moses.

Talk about the meaning of the passage. Ask: Why did Moses' mother hide him (refer to Ex. 1)? Why did Moses' sister take him to his mother?

Draw a picture of this biblical scene. Older children may wish to make a rebus, combining a story of the incident with pictures. Compare the pictures and display them in the place reserved for family worship.

Suggest that Mother recall the birth of each child in the family, emphasizing any unusual or difficult aspects of each birth.

Talk about sacrifices that parents sometimes make for their children. Note any sacrifices that parents of your family have made. Express appreciation for those sacrifices.

If there is a new baby in the family, talk about what each one can do to help train the child "in the way he should go" (Prov. 22:6).

If grandparents are living, plan a special expression

of love for them. Decide how each member of the family will participate.

Thank God for parents who love enough to make sacrifices for their children.

Death

Read John 11:1–45. Because of the length of this passage, take turns reading. One logical division of the passage is verses 1–16, 17–29, 30–37, 38–45.

In advance, ask someone to study this chapter in a Bible commentary and to report his findings to the family. Discuss the passage. Give special attention to verses 25–26. Ask: Do *you* believe this?

Ask: Why are most people reluctant to talk about death? Why do they try to avoid the subject? What did Paul mean when he wrote, "O death, where is thy sting? O grave, where is thy victory?" (1 Cor. 15:55). Why is death a victory celebration for the Christian?

Talk about a death in your family. Ask: Who or what brought you the most help and comfort in this experience? Did God seem nearer to you during this time? What part did prayer play in the experience?

Point out that much criticism is voiced today regarding the high cost of funerals and the commercialism surrounding death. Talk about how funerals can be made more helpful for the survivors.

Ask: How can our family minister to bereaved families? Consider these suggestions: visit, send sympathy messages, invite family for meals, send food, help with household chores, offer financial assistance. Add your own ideas to this list.

Plan some action the family will take to minister to a bereaved family. Include all the family in the project.

As a prayer, sing "He Lives."

Marriage

Read Genesis 1:26–28; 2:18,21–25. Talk about the meaning of the passage. Ask: Why is it best that a married couple leave father and mother? What is the meaning of "they shall be one flesh"? Assign this passage to someone to study in a Bible commentary and report to the family.

In advance, clip from a magazine a picture of a married couple. Then cut the picture into pieces to make a jigsaw puzzle. During worship, have the family put the puzzle together. Talk about how marriage is like fitting two lives together so that they blend into one.

Talk about happily married couples you know. Ask: What are the strengths of their marriage? What is the secret of their happiness?

Invite parents to talk about the strengths of their marriage. Suggest that each parent tell the other "some ways in which you help to make our marriage strong."

Invite the children to talk about the kind of marriage they want. Ask: How will you include God in your marriage plans?

If a member of the family is about to be married, invite him to share with the family how he will honor God in the new home.

As a prayer, sing "Bless This House, O Lord We Pray."

Sickness

Read Luke 9:37–42. Compare this passage with Matthew 17:14–20 and Mark 9:14–29. Talk about the meaning of the passage. Ask: How do you think the father felt when Jesus healed his son?

Talk about the ministry many churches have to the mute. If your church has such a ministry, talk about it and how your family may contribute to this ministry.

Does a member of the family know sign language? If he does, suggest that he demonstrate to the family and teach the others to "sign" a simple greeting or a Bible verse.

To demonstrate the difficulty the mute sometimes have in communicating, let members of the family take turns pantomiming familiar verses of Scripture. Let other members of the family see if they can "read" the verse by watching the gestures.

Suggest that Mother or Father recall a time when one of the children was seriously ill. Let them recall their feelings at the time and share them with the family. Ask: Did you pray? How did you pray? How were your prayers answered?

Plan a special activity to show loving concern for someone who is hospitalized or critically ill. Decide how each member of the family will participate.

Thank God for his healing power.

Separation

Read Matthew 12:46–50. Compare this passage with Mark 3:31–35 and Luke 8:19–21. Talk about the meaning of the passage. If you need help, refer to a Bible commentary. Give special attention to the meaning of verse 50.

Invite members of the family to talk about times when they left home and family, such as when they went away to school, to military service, on a trip, or other times. Ask: How did you feel? What did you miss most while you were away? How did you feel when you returned?

Is a member of the family preparing to leave home? Ask him what he will miss most about his home. How can the family make the separation easier for him?

Point out that Jesus' family at first did not understand his mission. They thought that he was "beside himself" (see Mark 3:21). Perhaps the reason they had come for him was to try to restore him to his senses.

Ask: Have you ever been misunderstood? How did you feel? What did you do about it? Has there ever been a time when your family misunderstood you? Did this hurt more than when others misunderstood? Why?

Say: The lesson Jesus taught was that while family ties and loyalties are strong, there are other commitments that may override one's commitment to home and family. What commitment did Jesus have that was stronger than his commitment to his family? Do we have ties that are even stronger than those binding us to home and family? What are they?

Pray for the faith and courage to put God first, even ahead of all earthly ties.

Homecoming or Reunion

Read Luke 15:11–32. Talk about the meaning of this passage. Discuss these questions: How do you feel toward the son who left home? toward the one who stayed at home? toward the father? Which one is most like you? Why did the son who stayed at home react as he did? Do you know a father as loving and forgiving as the one in the story?

Ask a member of the family to retell the story in his own words. You may prefer to act out the story with one member playing the part of the father, another the part of the son who left home, and a third the part of the son who stayed at home.

Write a story paralleling this one, but in a modern setting with modern characters. For example, a son or daughter may run away from home to join a commune or become involved in the drug culture. With smaller children, make a rebus or picture story using pictures clipped from magazines or hand-drawn figures to represent scenes from Jesus' story. Help the children to read their picture story.

Is a member of the family absent? Send him a message from the family. Plan a homecoming celebration upon his return. Include everyone in the preparation. You may wish to plan a family reunion. Agree on the time and place and assign responsibilities.

Think about this question: is there some incident, perhaps a quarrel or disagreement or misunderstanding, between a parent and child in your family? If the answer is yes, can the parent involved be as loving and forgiving as the father in this story?

Give thanks for a loving, forgiving heavenly Father, and pray that we may love others as he loves us.

Conversion

Read John 3:1–17. Assign this passage to someone in advance so that he may be prepared to read it to the family with feeling and expression. Stress that this is one of the most important passages ever recorded.

Recall that when President Carter told of his religious experience he used the term *born again*. Many news reporters were puzzled, for they had never heard the expression before. Talk about why *born again* is a graphic description of the conversion experience.

Invite each Christian present to retell his conversion experience. Some details that may be included are age at conversion, place, events that led to the experience, person or persons who were most helpful, what the experience meant, and highlights of your spiritual pilgrimage since conversion.

Invite the newest convert in the family to share his conversion experience and what it means to him.

Ask each Christian present to suggest at least one practice that he has found helpful in his Christian growth (prayer, Bible study, witnessing). Urge the newest convert to make his own list of practices that he will adopt to aid his growth as a Christian.

Talk about baptism as it was practiced in the New Testament. Conduct a quiz on the baptism of Jesus. Some questions to ask: Where was Jesus baptized? Why was he baptized? Who baptized him? How was he baptized? What evidence was there that his baptism pleased God (see Matt. 3:13–17)?

Sing prayerfully the chorus "For God So Loved the World." Pray that each Christian will be faithful to his commitment to Christ.

Celebration

Read Matthew 5:1–12. Compare the King James Version of this passage, known as the Beatitudes, with modern language translations of the Bible. Compare this passage with Luke 6:20–22. What does *beatitude* mean? Consult a dictionary.

Talk about the meaning of this passage. What was

Jesus saying to his disciples in these verses? What is he saying to us today?

Ask: What was the happiest day of your life? Give each member of the family opportunity to respond.

Recall the happiest day in the life of the family. Talk about other special days in the life of the family. What events seem to bring the most happiness to the family?

Ask: What kind of experiences make you happy? Encourage each member of the family to name several experiences or to make a list. Talk about how the kinds of experiences that make us happy reveal much about our character and the kinds of persons we are.

Write a paraphrase of the Beatitudes, putting the verses in your own language to express what the words mean to you. This paraphrase may be written individually or as a family. Preschoolers will need help, but school children and youth may be encouraged to write their own.

Think about others in your church, neighborhood, and community. How can your family help to make someone else happy? Plan a project that will bring joy and happiness to another—perhaps a shut-in, someone sick or hospitalized, a lonely person, or someone who is experiencing grief or sorrow. Decide what part each member of the family will have in carrying out the project.

Pray for the merry heart that does more good for ills than medicine (Prov. 17:22) and that you will share your joy with others.

Index

Old Testament Family Life

The Life and Teachings of Jesus

The Royal Law of Family Life

For Holidays and Special Occasions